Snap books®

Endangered and Threatened Animals

AFRICAN ELEPHANTS

by Brenda Haugen

Consultant:
Gay Bradshaw, PhD
Director of the Kerulos Center
Jacksonville, Oregon

CAPSTONE PRESS
a capstone imprint

Snap Books are published by Capstone Press,
1710 Roe Crest Drive, North Mankato, Minnesota 56003.
www.capstonepub.com

Library of Congress Cataloging-in-Publication Data
Haugen, Brenda.
  African elephants / by Brenda Haugen.
    p. cm. — (Snap Books. Endangered and threatened animals.)
  Includes bibliographical references and index.
  Summary: "Describes the life cycle and characteristics of African elephants, including physical and environmental threats to the species"—Provided by publisher.
  ISBN 978-1-4296-8664-8 (library binding)
  ISBN 978-1-62065-344-9 (ebook PDF)
  1. African elephant—Juvenile literature. 2. Endangered species—Juvenile literature. I. Title.

  QL737.P98H38 2013
  599.67'4—dc23   2012000036

Editor: Mari Bolte
Designer: Bobbie Nuytten
Media Researcher: Marcie Spence
Production Specialist: Kathy McColley

Photo Credits:
Alamy: blickwinkel, 6 (bottom), 7 (right); Capstone: 10; Corbis: Joseph Sohm/Visions of America, 28; Kim Lukaszka, 27, 29; Shutterstock: Alberto Tirado, 21 (top), Amelandfoto, 13, Andy Dean Photography, 17, Anke van Wyk, 6 (top), Arve Bettum, 21 (bottom), Debbie Aird Photography, 19, Dudarev Mikhail, 25 (pollution), elfart, 25 (habitat), Four Oaks, 12, galal, 15, Jason Prince, 11, Johan Swanepoel, 22, 24, Laurent Renault, 25 (globe), Lucian Coman, 25 (habitat and gun), Oleg Znamenskiy, design element, ostill, cover, palko72, 18, patrimonio designs unlimited, design element, PhotoSky.com, 23, Robert Hardolt, 7 (left)

Printed in the United States of America in North Mankato, Minnesota.
042012   006682CGF12

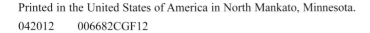

Table of Contents

Chapter 1

We Are Family

The hot African sun rises high in the sky. Waves of moist heat lift from the **savanna** into the air above. But despite the heat, the rolling grassland dotted with trees is full of life. In the tall grass, a herd of zebras grazes, watchful for **carnivores** such as lions, wild dogs, and hyenas. In the distance, a herd of wildebeests also munches lazily on the green grass.

Nearby, a family of elephants frolics in the cool of a muddy river. Some of the elephants suck water up in their huge trunks. They spray the water onto their backs. Others playfully squirt water at one another.

After their bath, the elephants cover their skin with mud or dust. This coat protects the elephants from insects and the burning sun. Elephant skin looks rough, but an elephant's skin, face, ears, and trunk are sensitive.

But elephants face threats greater than biting bugs or high temperatures. Millions of elephants once roamed over all of Africa. Sport hunting, **poaching,** and **habitat** loss have cut the population to a fraction of what it once was. Between 1979 and 1989, the elephant population dropped from 1.2 million to 600,000. Today only a few small groups of elephants remain in Africa. Scientists believe that, without help, this magnificent species may disappear in the next 20 years.

savanna: a flat, grassy area of land with few or no trees

carnivore: an animal that hunts other animals for food

poaching: the act of hunting or fishing illegally

habitat: the natural place and conditions in which a plant or animal lives

There are two types of African elephants—savanna elephants and forest elephants. Forest elephants are smaller than savanna elephants. Their tusks are straighter, and their ears are oval-shaped. Forest elephants also live in smaller family groups. They typically live in the forests of Africa.

Savanna elephant: Height: 12 feet (3.7 meters) at the shoulder
Length: 25 feet (7.6 m)
Weight: 14,000 pounds (6,350 kilograms)

Forest elephant: Height: 8 feet (2.4 m) at the shoulder
Length: 13 feet (4 m)
Weight: 6,000 pounds (2,700 kg)

Savanna elephants are the world's largest land mammals.

12 feet
(3.7 m)

8 feet
(2.4 m)

6 feet
(1.8 m)

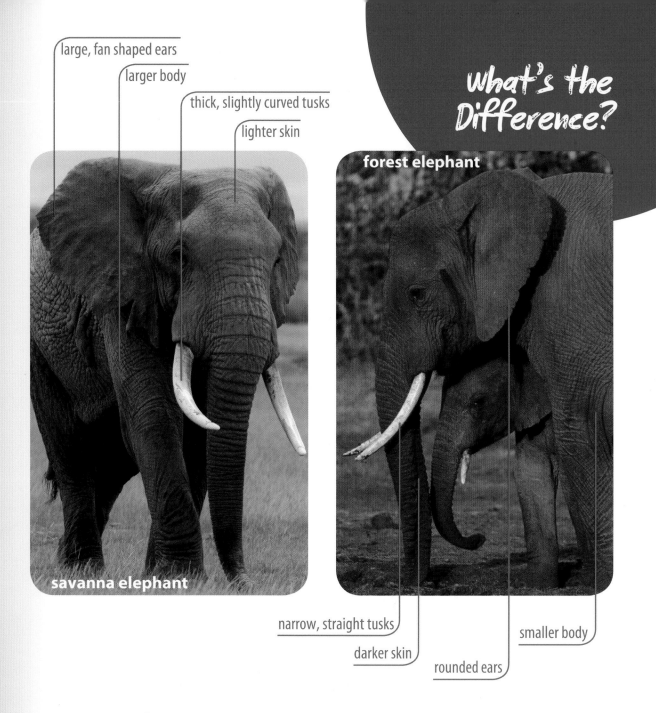

large, fan shaped ears

larger body

thick, slightly curved tusks

lighter skin

forest elephant

savanna elephant

narrow, straight tusks

darker skin

rounded ears

smaller body

Both species are at risk. Under the Endangered Species Act, the African elephant is listed as threatened. Threatened animals are at risk of becoming endangered in the near future. Today only about 500,000 savanna elephants and 40,000 forest elephants live in the wild.

Chapter 2

The Life of an Elephant

Some of Africa's elephants live on savannas. Others live in dry woodland areas south of the Sahara Desert. Still others are found in mountains or dense tropical rain forests.

Elephants play an important role in their **ecosystem**. They spread seeds from a variety of plants and trees. Their huge bodies brush against trees and plants, causing nuts and seeds to fall. The nuts and seeds provide food for other, smaller animals. The seeds eaten by elephants are spread to new areas through the elephants' manure.

Elephants provide water for other animals too. They dig holes in dry riverbeds searching for something to drink. Once they're no longer thirsty, they leave the watery hole behind. And their huge footprints trap rainwater for other animals to drink.

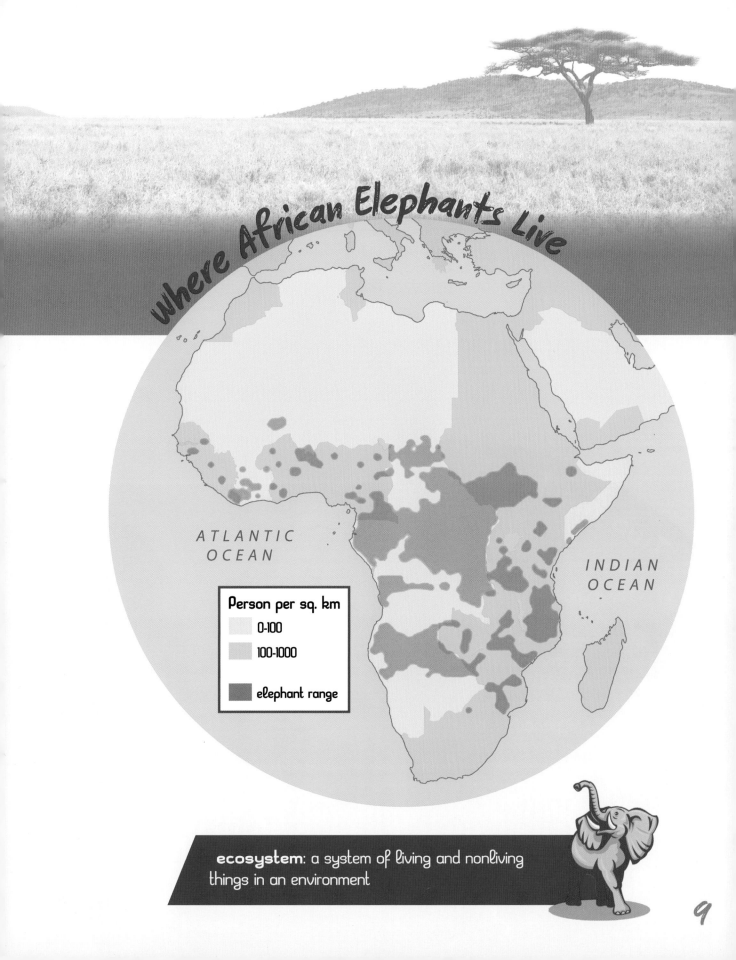

Where African Elephants Live

ATLANTIC OCEAN

INDIAN OCEAN

Person per sq. km
0-100
100-1000
elephant range

ecosystem: a system of living and nonliving things in an environment

Both male and female elephants have tusks that they use for defense. But tusks are mainly used as tools. They can be used to dig for water, pry bark off trees, and lift large items.

Like people, elephants tend to favor one side over the other. You can tell if an elephant is right- or left-tusked by looking at the elephant's tusk size. The favored tusk will be smaller and more worn down.

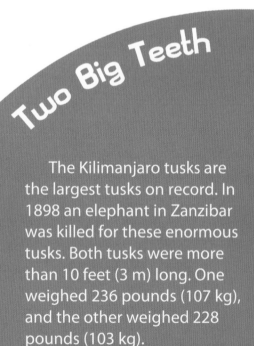

Two Big Teeth

The Kilimanjaro tusks are the largest tusks on record. In 1898 an elephant in Zanzibar was killed for these enormous tusks. Both tusks were more than 10 feet (3 m) long. One weighed 236 pounds (107 kg), and the other weighed 228 pounds (103 kg).

Elephants use their trunks like humans use their hands. Trunk are used to touch and greet other elephants. Elephants are able to recognize hundreds of other elephants through smell, touch, sight, and sound. An elephant's trunk has about 15,000 muscles, and is about 7 feet (2 m) long. That's about 20 times more than the human body.

Trunk Talk

Elephants make a variety of sounds with their trunks to communicate. They have different sounds for happiness, excitement, or anger. An elephant's trumpet can be heard up to 5 miles (8 km) away.

Trunks are also used for moving water and drinking. Adult elephants can suck up 2 gallons (7.6 liters) of water in their trunks at one time. When elephants want to drink, they curl their trunks toward their mouths. Then they stick the tip into their mouths and blow. The water shoots right down their throats. Elephants drink about 30 gallons (114 L) of water each day.

Elephants can breathe through both their mouths and trunks.

Elephants don't chew their meals. Instead they move their molars in a back-and-forth motion to grind their food.

Along with roots and bark, elephants eat grass, leaves, shrubs, and fruit. Elephants eat around 300 to 600 pounds (136 to 272 kg) of food each day. They use their giant molars to grind down their food. Elephants have four molars—two on top and two on the bottom. Each molar is about the size of a brick and can weigh as much as 5 pounds (2.3 kg). An elephant may go through six sets of molars in its lifetime.

Elephants have strong family ties. A typical family includes eight to 15 related female elephants. Elephant calves are cared for by their mothers. Females without their own calves, called allomothers, also help raise young elephants.

The matriarch leads the family. The matriarch is usually one of the oldest, most experienced females of the family. She uses her life experience to guide the other elephants. She helps them find food and water and watches for danger.

Elephants need lots of space. The group may travel in an area of 850 square miles (2,200 square kilometers) while searching for food and water. Elephants **migrate** along ancient routes as the seasons change. When the dry season approaches, the savanna grass begins to die.

The family spends the summer near rivers and other water sources that don't dry up. There, they meet up with other families. They also connect with all-male herds to mate. In the fall, heavy rains arrive. The elephants return to places where the grass is rich and green.

During the dry season, small family groups meet other elephants and form large herds with more than 100 members.

However, the ancient routes elephants follow are being blocked off. Humans build cities, farms, and roads in the elephants' paths. Whole groups are cut off from their relatives.

To fix this problem, parks and **reserves** have been set up throughout Africa. Some act as bridges between farmland, allowing elephants to migrate freely and safely. But more people in elephant territory means more contact between the two species.

migrate: to travel from one area to another on a regular basis

reserve: land that is protected so that animals may live there safely

Growing Up and Growing Old

Chapter 3

Elephants live a long time. But they also take a long time to be born—nearly two years. An elephant's **gestation period** lasts about 22 months. Females reach maturity between 9 and 14 years old. They can have a calf every four or five years. Baby elephants are usually born in the fall, at the beginning of the rainy season.

Newborn elephants stand 3 feet (1 m) at the shoulder. They weigh more than 200 pounds (91 kg). Like all mammals, elephant calves need their mother's milk—and a lot of it! A calf can drink 10 gallons (38 L) of milk each day.

Calves stay very close to their mothers and the allomothers. The African savanna is a dangerous place. Lions, crocodiles, leopards, and jaguars are only a few of the animals that prey on baby elephants.

gestation period: the amount of time an unborn animal spends inside its mother

Elephant Life Cycle

- calf is born after a 22 month gestation period

- 9 months old: elephant's teeth begin to grow in; grasses and small branches become part of the diet

- 1 year old: begins to eat more and more vegetation

- 12–14 months old: elephant still considered a baby

- 4–5 years old: calf is weaned from mother's milk

- 10 years old: females reach maturity

- 10–12 years old: males leave to join all-male herds or live alone

- 20–30 years old: males reach maturity

- 50–60 years old: elephants reach the end of their lives

Mothers, allomothers, and older siblings teach young calves what to eat and where to find food. Calves are also taught how to communicate with other elephants. This constant contact strengthens the bond within the family.

Young elephants reach maturity in their early teens. Females stay with the herd their whole lives. Males leave the family between the ages of 10 and 12. They will live on their own or with a group of other male elephants.

Elephants reach middle age near their 30th year. As elephants near 60 years old, the fine hair on their heads may turn a silvery gray. Their skin becomes more wrinkled. Their ears may become more frayed at the edges. Their teeth begin to wear down, making eating difficult. These are all signs an elephant is nearing death.

Elderly elephants often move to marshy areas with soft, easy-to-chew grasses.

Elephant Sadness

Like humans, elephants experience grief and loss. Because they live for so long, elephants can form relationships that last for decades. The loss of a family member is difficult. Scientists have noticed behavior changes in elephants after illness or death of another elephant. The death of a matriarch is especially hard.

Chapter 4

A Threatened Animal

Humans are the only threat to elephants' survival. Elephants have been hunted for their tusks, meat, and hides since Europe began colonizing Africa in the late 1800s. Before that time, people and elephants lived in a peaceful co-existence. But by the 1970s, the demand for tusk ivory resulted in the killing of millions of elephants.

Without the ivory ban that was passed in the 1980s, elephants might be extinct today. But the hunting still continues. More than 38,000 elephants are poached every year. A poacher in Zimbabwe may face up to a $20,000 fine. However, one tusk can bring in around $1,000. To some, the risk is worth it.

Poaching a single elephant harms the entire elephant family. When a matriarch is killed, the family loses her valuable knowledge. They also experience grief over the loss of an important family leader.

Ivory in the News

The year 2011 has been called the worst year for elephants since the ivory ban. Nearly 26 tons (23.7 metric tons) of smuggled ivory was seized that year. To compare, less than 11 tons (10 metric tons) of ivory was found the year before. In most cases, the ivory was being smuggled from Africa to Asia.

Experts estimate that more than 2,500 elephants were killed for their ivory in 2011. One park in Kenya has been losing 100 elephants a year to poaching.

- In April, 707 tusks and 32 ivory bracelets were seized in China. The items were valued at about $15 million. Just two weeks earlier, 247 tusks had been uncovered in Thailand. They were hidden with frozen fish shipped from Kenya.

- In August, officials in Hong Kong seized 794 pieces of African ivory. The tusks weighed nearly 4,400 pounds (2,000 kg) and were worth $1.6 million.

- In December, hundreds of tusks valued at $1.3 million were found. They were hidden with a shipment of handcrafted goods from Kenya.

More than 1 billion people live in Africa. And that number keeps growing. Africa has the highest birth rate of any other continent. In the next 40 years, the population is expected to double in size.

As the population grows, towns and cities grow too. Farmers plant more food to feed the people. This growth means that there's less land for elephants, who are forced from their homes.

Human developments such as farms, roads, and houses block the migration routes that elephants have traveled for thousands of years. They cannot get to their regular food sources. To avoid starvation, they eat farm crops. Angry people try to chase the elephants away. Sometimes they kill an elephant. Other times, an elephant protecting its calf accidentally kills or injures a person.

The confrontation between humans and elephants is called the Human-Elephant Conflict (HEC).

In addition to being harmful to elephants, elephant fences can be expensive and hard to maintain.

Some people use chili pepper to protect their homes. The elephants don't care for the pepper smell and stay away. Others build fences to keep elephants out. While the fences often work, they're also dangerous. Baby elephants can get caught in the fences and die. Adults who get caught risk deep cuts, which may lead to infection. And gentle elephants caught in fences make easy targets for hunters.

Like all of Earth's creatures, elephants are now also in danger from **global warming**. In Africa temperatures climb and rainfall decreases. Droughts become more common. Elephants depend on rainfall for drinking water. The rainfall also helps their food sources grow. But drought and human development mean that elephants have fewer places to go to find water and food.

Many elephants die in droughts. Ambolesi National Park in Kenya recorded huge losses in 2008 and 2009. A drought, coupled with poaching, killed nearly 400 of the park's 1,550 elephants. Ninety-five percent of the matriarchs died, making the loss even more shocking.

Scientists have found that global warming is affecting elephant reproduction. Hungry elephants have a harder time getting pregnant.

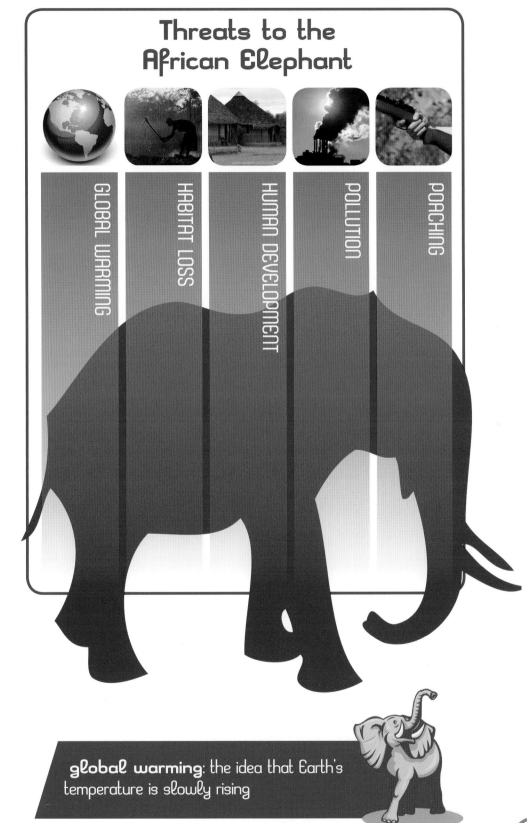

Threats to the African Elephant

GLOBAL WARMING

HABITAT LOSS

HUMAN DEVELOPMENT

POLLUTION

POACHING

global warming: the idea that Earth's temperature is slowly rising

Chapter 5

Saving the African Giant

Hannah Wright remembers the sound of herds of elephants trumpeting in the night. "Elephants were probably 200 feet (61 m) from our tent. It was insane. You walked out and could hear them roaring," she said.

Hannah, a North Dakota teen, spent time at a refuge center in Africa. There, she helped care for orphaned baby elephants. Most had fallen in wells and were brought to the refuge. "It was really sad, but they're helping them at the refuge center. Then they release them back in the wild later, so that was really cool," Hannah said.

Want to Learn More?

Check out some of these great conservation groups to learn more about elephants and what you can do to help.

*The David Sheldrick Wildlife Trust

* Animal Rights Africa

*The Kerulos Center

*In Defense of Animals

Orphan elephants raised in a sanctuary or refuge center are given the chance to grow up in a safe environment.

Although you may never make it to Africa, there are way you can help the elephants. Learn all you can about conservation and wildlife protection. Find out how to share the environment with other species. Read all you can about elephants, and share this information with friends and family. The more people know about an animal, the more they'll want to help.

Get together with your friends to raise money for your favorite elephant-related organization. Groups such as the World Wildlife Fund and the David Sheldrick Wildlife Trust give donors the chance to adopt or foster elephants in need.

Organizations around the world work to protect the future of elephants.

Young elephants won't have the knowledge to survive without older elephants to learn from.

You can help endangered animals like the elephant no matter what your age or geographic location. The efforts of kids like you are helping save the elephant every day. But there's still a lot to do! Don't be afraid to make a difference. The future of the elephant depends on you.

Glossary

carnivore (KAHR-nuh-vohr)—an animal that hunts other animals for food

ecosystem (EE-koh-sis-tuhm)—a system of living and nonliving things in an environment

endangered (in-DAYN-juhrd)—at risk of dying out

extinct (ik-STINGKT)—no longer living; an extinct animal is one that has died out with no more of its kind

gestation period (je-STAY-shuhn PIHR-ee-uhd)—the amount of time an unborn animal spends inside its mother

global warming (GLOH-buhl WAWRM-ing)—the idea that Earth's temperature is slowly rising

habitat (HAB-uh-tat)—the natural place and conditions in which a plant or animal lives

matriarch (MAY-tree-ark)—a female who rules or dominates a family or group

migrate (MYE-grate)—to travel from one area to another on a regular basis

orphan (OR-fuhn)—a young animal that has lost its mother

poaching (POHCH-ing)—the act of hunting or fishing illegally

reserve (ri-ZURV)—land that is protected so that animals may live there safely

savanna (suh-VAN-uh)—a flat, grassy area of land with few or no trees

seize (SEEZ)—the act of taking something away from someone

smuggle (SMUHG-uhl)—to move something secretly and often illegally

Read More

Allen, Kathy. *Elephants Under Pressure: A Cause and Effect Investigation*. Animals on the Edge. Mankato, Minn.: Capstone Press, 2011.

Brennan, Francis. *Elephants*. Nature's Children. New York: Children's Press, 2013.

O'Connell, Caitlin, and Donna M. Jackson. *The Elephant Scientist*. Boston: Houghton Mifflin Books for Children, 2011.

Internet Sites

FactHound offers a safe, fun way to find Internet sites related to this book. All of the sites on FactHound have been researched by our staff.

Here's all you do:

Visit *www.facthound.com*

Type in this code: 9781429686648

Super-cool stuff! Check out projects, games and lots more at www.capstonekids.com

Index

allomothers, 14, 16, 18
Ambolesi National Park, 24

carnivores, 4
conservation groups, 26, 28

droughts, 24

elephants
    calves, 14, 16, 17, 18, 22, 27
    communication, 11, 14, 18
    diet, 8, 13, 14, 16, 17, 18, 22, 24
    ears, 6, 18
    emotion, 19, 20
    families, 4, 6, 14, 15, 18, 19, 20
    gestation, 16, 24
    life cycle, 17, 18
    orphans, 26, 27
    and people, 5, 15, 20, 21, 22,
        23, 26
    population of, 5, 7
    range, 6, 8
    size, 6, 16
    skin, 4, 18
    sounds, 11, 26
    teeth, 13, 17, 18

threats to, 5, 15, 16, 20, 22, 23, 25
trunks, 4, 11, 12
tusks, 6, 10, 20, 21
types of, 6, 7
Endangered Species Act, 7

global warming, 4, 25

habitats
    forests, 6, 7, 8
    savannas, 4, 6, 7, 8, 14, 16

ivory ban, 20, 21

Kilimanjaro tusks, 10

matriarchs, 14, 19, 20, 24
migration, 14, 15, 22

poaching, 5, 20, 21, 23, 24

refuge centers, 26, 27, 28
reserves, 15

water, 4, 8, 10, 12, 14, 24